For my father, Patrick J. Conlon, who
first told me about 'unicorns'
MC-M

For my family and friends
CC

First U.S. Edition

First published in Great Britain by ABC, All Books for Children,
a division of The All Children's Company Ltd.,
33 Museum Street, London WC1A 1LD, England

ISBN 0-316-54781-6

Library of Congress Catalog Card Number 94-76977

10 9 8 7 6 5 4 3 2 1

Published simultaneously in Canada
by Little, Brown & Company (Canada) Limited

Printed in Hong Kong

The Very Last Unicorn

Written by Marita Conlon–McKenna

Illustrated by Chris Coady

 Little, Brown and Company
Boston New York Toronto London

It was on a snowy morning that Sam
first looked out and saw the unicorn standing
there, alone and cold, its head bent low. After
pulling on his jacket, his warm, woolly hat
and gloves, and his big yellow boots, Sam
raced outside.

The chill air burned his nose, and his breath
formed clouds that hung still. He stared at the
unicorn, and the unicorn stared right back at
him. Looking so white and proud, with eyes
of green and a magical tilted horn, the unicorn
stomped on the ground, trying
to keep warm as the snowflakes
feathered all around.

"I am the one and only, the very last
unicorn in the world."
"Oh!" said Sam.
"I am lonely, and I need a home.
I have nowhere to go."

Sam thought of his small room.
"I know somewhere you can
hear the lions roar."

Sam led the unicorn to the town zoo. "It's full
of animals and birds here. They are safe, and
hundreds of people come to see them."
The unicorn seemed to understand.

Animals paced up and down behind wires and
bars and cages. Monkeys chattered and parakeets
screeched as the unicorn walked among them.

"I would have food and shelter here?"
"Yes!" said Sam.
"And thousands would come to see me?"
"Millions!"

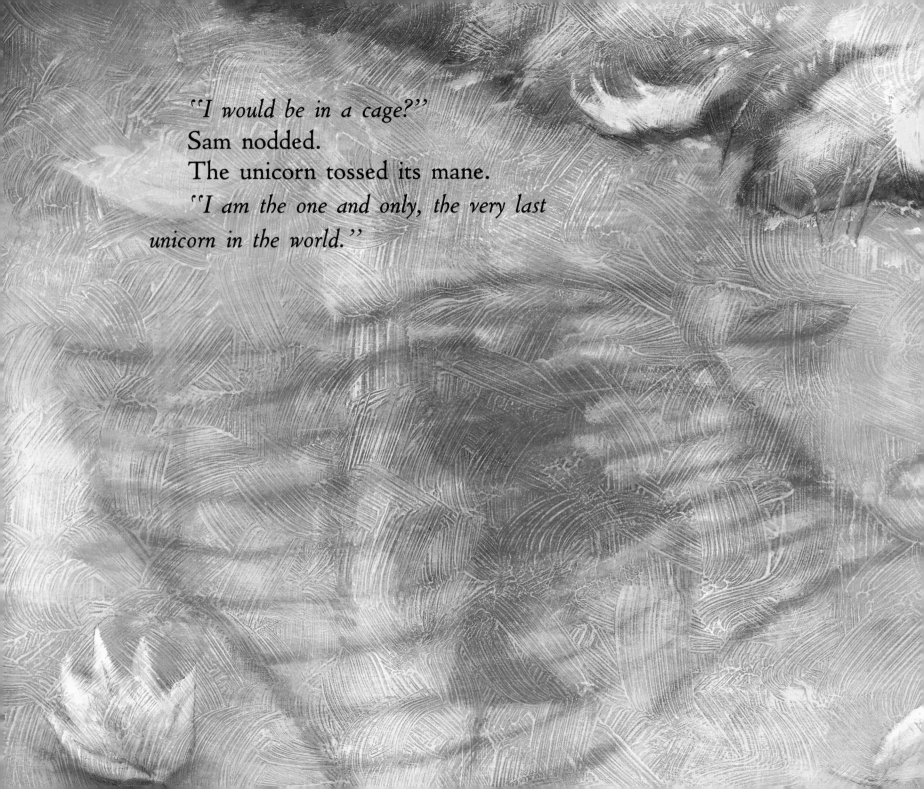

"I would be in a cage?"
Sam nodded.
The unicorn tossed its mane.
"I am the one and only, the very last
unicorn in the world."

"I know," said Sam,
and they walked on.
They wandered through a maze of
streets, not knowing where to go. The unicorn
was sad and weary as they searched for a home.

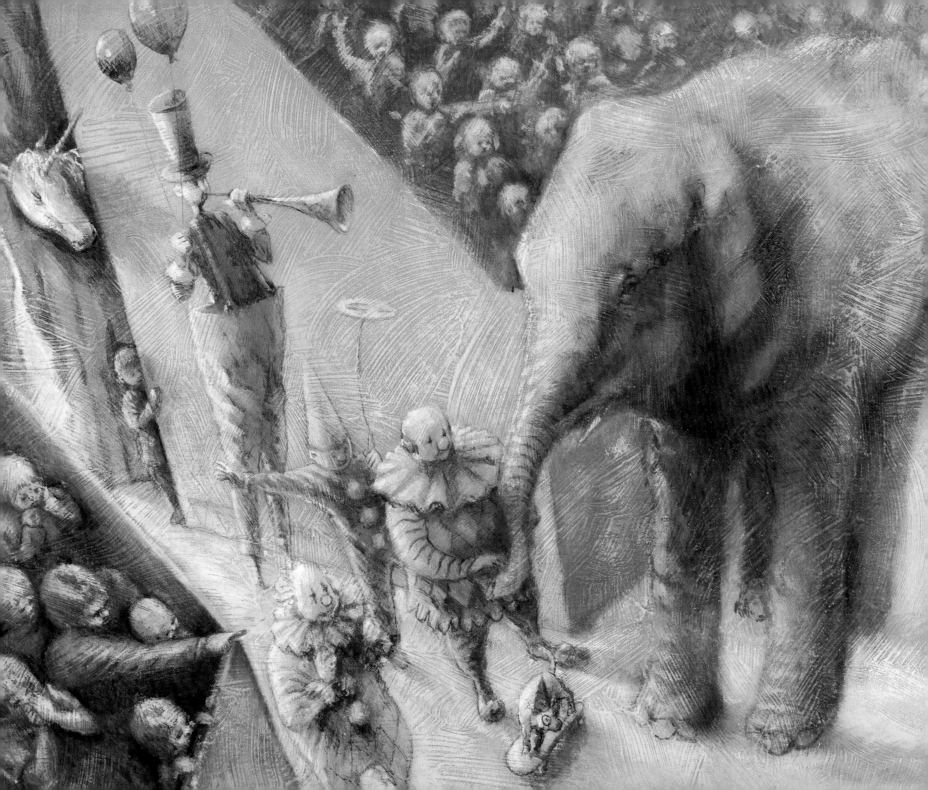

Ahead of them, bright-colored flags
fluttered in the breeze.

"It's a circus!" cried Sam. They slipped inside
the tent, and the unicorn hid in the shadows. Clowns
and jugglers tumbled as one act followed another.
The unicorn pricked up its ears as a beautiful
black horse pranced around and around the ring.

"If you joined the circus, you'd go
from town to town, and everyone would
cheer for you," said Sam.

"*From town to town?*"

"Yes." Sam stroked the unicorn's nose.

"*I am the one and only, the very last unicorn in the world.*"

"I know," said Sam, and they walked on.

The snow was melting to slush as the sun tried to shine. They walked along a lonely road, passing gardens and orchards and fields and farmyards.

"My grandfather lives near here. There's a forest and a stream and mountains."

Suddenly, in the distance, a group of wild ponies appeared. They lifted their heads and neighed. "Yes, there they are!" laughed Sam.

The ponies' tails and manes were tangled, and their coats were shaggy. But their eyes were bright, and they tossed their heads high. The unicorn stood still, watching them.

Sam patted the unicorn. Flecks of wet mud clung to the animal's white hair.

"I am the one and only, the very last unicorn in the world."

"I know," said Sam. He hugged the unicorn's neck.

The ponies called again.
"Go!" said Sam. "It's safe here.
I'll visit you."

The unicorn took one step, then two, then trotted toward the ponies.

It was getting late. Sam's mother would be worried. He had to hurry home. He stared and stared, to make sure that he would never forget, and as he waved he caught his breath.

For suddenly there was not one but a whole group of unicorns running through the woods. "I know," said Sam, and he walked on.